TAMI LEWIS BROWN ◆ PICTURES BY FRANÇOIS ROCA

Soar, Elinor!

FARRAR STRAUS GIROUX

NEW YORK

To Melanie Kroupa, who helped me and this book soar
—T.L.B.

To my two daughters, Suzanne and Angèle
—F.R.

In 1917, some girls dressed their dolls. They played house and hopscotch, jump rope and jacks.

But one little girl wanted more. Elinor Smith was born to soar.

Six-year-old Elinor read a sign posted in a Long Island potato field: AIRPLANE RIDES—$5 AND $10.

Flimsy as a box kite, the Farman pusher biplane coughed and rumbled across the field. Elinor begged her father to let her hop aboard.

Five dollars bought a week's groceries in those days, and rickety flying machines were dangerous. But Elinor's father knew what it was to have a dream. He was a vaudeville showman who danced on Broadway.

And Tom Smith knew his daughter. So he knotted her blond braids together to keep them from blowing in the wind, and lifted Elinor and her little brother, Joe, into the cockpit, fastening the seat belt around them both.

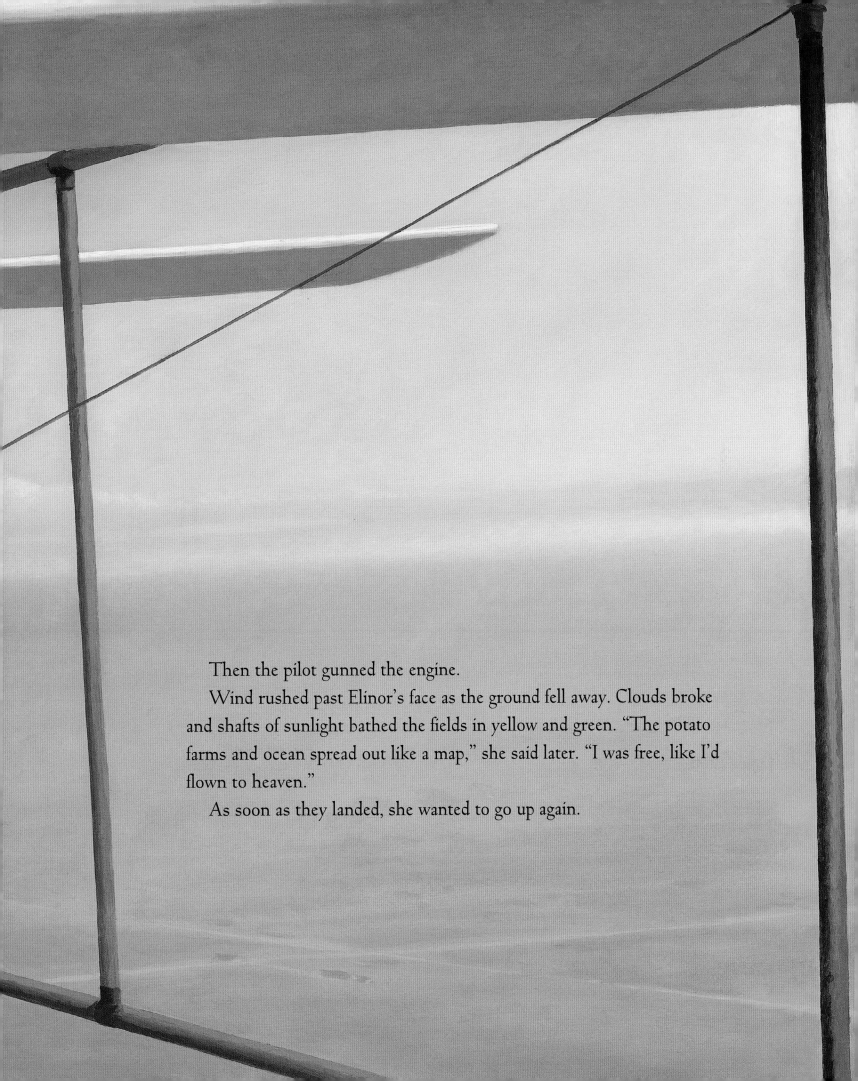

Then the pilot gunned the engine.

Wind rushed past Elinor's face as the ground fell away. Clouds broke and shafts of sunlight bathed the fields in yellow and green. "The potato farms and ocean spread out like a map," she said later. "I was free, like I'd flown to heaven."

As soon as they landed, she wanted to go up again.

When Elinor was ten, she began flying lessons. Her teacher strapped blocks to the rudder bar so her feet could reach it, then taught her how to guide the control stick. To Elinor, the engine's exhaust was a spicy perfume.

"She will fly one day with the great ones," an old pilot said. "She has the touch."

At fifteen, Elinor thought she was ready to fly alone. Her father said no. She had to wait until she was eighteen.

But Elinor's mother knew what it was to have a dream, too. When she was a girl, she had hoped to have a singing career, but her parents wouldn't give her voice lessons.

And Agnes Smith knew her daughter. "If flying airplanes is what you want to do," she said, "be like the U.S. Mail. Don't let rain, sleet, or snow deter you."

So Mrs. Smith hired a new instructor, Russ Holderman, and Elinor began to train for her solo flight. Every morning, Elinor woke before sunrise, pulled on her brother's knickers and old leather jacket, and headed to the airfield to meet her teacher.

She practiced takeoffs and landings. Pilots call them touch and goes. She landed her plane, tapped the ground for a moment, then slammed the throttle to the wall and climbed back into the sky.

She did this over and over, until it was time to park her plane and head off to school.

Soar, Elinor, soar!

One day, Mr. Holderman climbed out of the cockpit. "Take her around,"
he said. "She's all yours."

Elinor hesitated. She'd learned to land only ten days before. Was she ready
to fly alone? "It's now or never," she thought as she taxied down the runway.

She climbed to 1,000 feet and leveled off. "In that instant," she said, "I knew I
was home and would never turn back." She practiced banking turns, then glided
in to land with a gentle bump.

She had done it! She had soloed!

From that moment, Elinor lived to fly. The sky was her playing field; the hum of the wind rushing through her plane's wing wires, her favorite song.

She flew upside down, right side up, and sideways. She learned to handle fire in the engine, ice on the wings, and fog-filled skies. She practiced emergency landings in grassy fields, along sandy beaches, and on the water.

Finally, in August 1928, Elinor earned her pilot's license. At sixteen, she was the youngest flier in the United States—boy or girl.

Soar, soar, Elinor!

But not everyone thought Elinor should fly.

Girls shouldn't mess with machines, some people claimed. Airplanes are for men and boys. Newspapers wrote that Elinor was just playing at being a pilot. They called her the Flying Flapper.

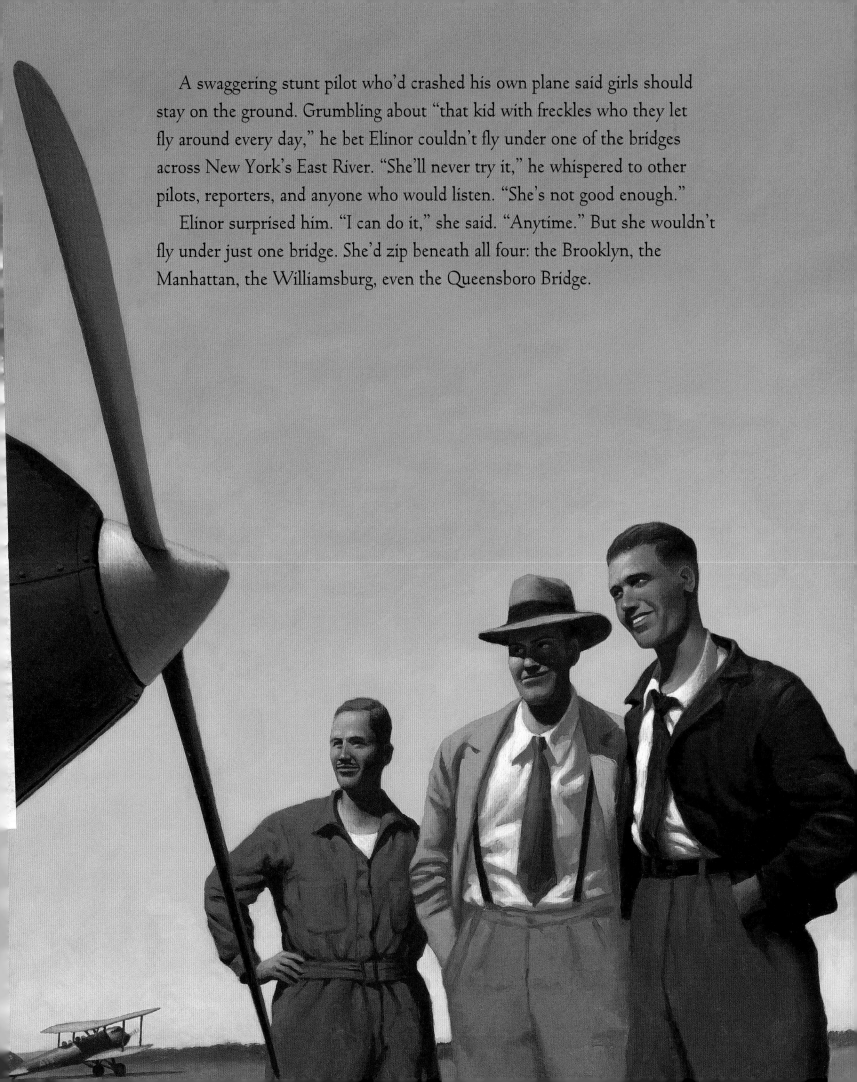

A swaggering stunt pilot who'd crashed his own plane said girls should stay on the ground. Grumbling about "that kid with freckles who they let fly around every day," he bet Elinor couldn't fly under one of the bridges across New York's East River. "She'll never try it," he whispered to other pilots, reporters, and anyone who would listen. "She's not good enough."

Elinor surprised him. "I can do it," she said. "Anytime." But she wouldn't fly under just one bridge. She'd zip beneath all four: the Brooklyn, the Manhattan, the Williamsburg, even the Queensboro Bridge.

No one had ever flown a plane under all four bridges. Flying under any bridge was dangerous. Swirling gusts of wind could slam a small plane into a bridge's stone pillars. Flying under bridges was also illegal. The government could take her license away, and flying was her life.

Careful planning was her answer. Elinor visited New York City and inspected every inch of her route. "I hung by my heels from all those bridges," she joked, "checking everything out." She calculated speed, distance, and weight, and studied tide tables and the design of each bridge.

Her nimble plane, a Waco 10, had a wingspan short enough to slip between the bridge footings. Skimming the water's surface over Manhasset Bay, she practiced by weaving through ship masts like a skier attacking a slalom course.

Finally Elinor was ready. She'd fly low, just above the East River, beneath every one of the four bridges. And she'd fly slow, too, barely above a stall. She thought that she'd planned for every possibility. Still, what if a gust of wind smashed her into a bridge support or a ship blocked her way?

On Sunday, October 21, 1928, Elinor slipped on her lucky sneakers and a red leather jacket—easy to spot if she crashed into the river and had to be fished out. She was just seventeen.

As she prepared for takeoff from Roosevelt Field, someone tapped on the cockpit. It was the world-famous pilot Charles Lindbergh, the first to fly solo across the Atlantic Ocean, nonstop. "Good luck, kid," he said. "Keep your nose down on the turns."

Elinor flew down the river, scanning for hazards. The water glimmered silver and white. Over her shoulder she saw the trees and green fields of Central Park. Sunlight and shadows played among Manhattan's tall buildings.

Then something surprised her. Near the southern tip of the island of Manhattan, the Brooklyn and Manhattan bridges huddled closer to one another than she had expected. Starting here, from the south, would be like threading the eye of a needle, even in the little Waco. Palms sweating, Elinor changed her plans and headed back up the river. She would start from the Queensboro Bridge, flying north to south, saving the toughest part for last.

The Queensboro Bridge reached across the water, wide and sturdy, its foundation carved of gray stone and its structure a tapestry of steel. As she flew closer, Elinor spotted someone waving a white scarf from the bridge deck. A newsreel reporter! Now the government would have proof, captured on film, that she'd flown under the bridges. Would they use the newsreels against her to take away her license?

One thing was certain. This flight had to be perfect. She wagged her wings to salute the film crew and pushed the stick forward.

Elinor had calculated the clearance between river and bridge, but as she ducked beneath the Queensboro she was in for another surprise. Heavy wooden blocks dangled from ropes tied to the bridge deck.

She held her breath, pointed the Waco's nose down, and dove toward the water, nearly kissing its surface. She weaved between the blocks, just as she'd practiced with the ship masts, and zipped out the other side.

Elinor flew on toward the Williamsburg Bridge. The motor seemed to growl, deep and low, as she pulled back on the throttle and slipped down to the water. Waves almost lapped her plane's belly.

Slow and steady, Elinor glided beneath the bridge. Just ahead, the Manhattan Bridge hovered before her. It seemed to float above the water from a grid of thick cables. Streetcars ran along the top deck, automobiles on the bottom.

Elinor waved to spectators, then dipped beneath the bridge. A nudge to the throttle and she made it through.

Now there was only one more bridge. There it was, just a few yards
ahead, its huge granite towers rising from the murky waters: the Brooklyn
Bridge. Some say the Brooklyn Bridge is New York's greatest bridge. That
day it was Elinor Smith's greatest challenge.

Elinor had considered currents, airspeed, and fuel. But she couldn't plan
for river traffic. A tanker chugged beneath the bridge. Elinor thought her little
Waco would have enough space. Then, as she swooped down toward the
bridge, Elinor saw something else: a Navy destroyer plowing toward her.

Tanker on the left, destroyer on the right. They filled the river and the
air beneath the bridge, leaving little room for Elinor.

Could she squeeze between the ships?

She yanked the control stick, tipped the wings, and flipped her plane into a vertical bank.
Elinor Smith flew under the Brooklyn Bridge—sideways!

She had pulled it off. She had flown under all four bridges.
Elinor circled the Statue of Liberty as boats in the harbor shot up
plumes of water and blew their whistles in salute.

Soar, soar, Elinor!

Then she headed home to Long Island, the crisp fall breeze swirling around her tiny Waco. Elinor flew over the patchwork of Long Island potato fields, where she'd practiced for her flight under the bridges, where she'd soloed and earned her pilot's license, and where, eleven years before, she'd climbed aboard an airplane for the very first time.

She came in for a perfect landing, and a crowd surrounded her—her mother, her father, her brother Joe, famous pilots and reporters, and dozens of others.

"Hooray!" they cheered, congratulating Elinor with hugs and pats on the back.

But what would the New York City officials think, or the Department of Commerce in Washington, D.C.? Would they take her license away?

New York City Mayor Jimmy Walker called Elinor to his office. Heart pounding and stomach tied in knots, she listened as he told her that he admired her bravery, but that she'd broken the law. Then he issued her a short suspension from flying. A few months later, he asked Elinor to name a plane in the city's honor—and she did.

Soon, Elinor got a letter from the Department of Commerce.

They told her to stop flying under bridges—but tucked inside the official letter was a handwritten note asking for her autograph!

Her license was safe.

With her plucky spirit and lots of hard work, Elinor had achieved more than anyone thought possible. She was a real pilot now, a professional aviator.

She'd shown the world what a girl could do—

Soar!

AUTHOR'S NOTE

BY THE TIME ELINOR LANDED AT ROOSEVELT FIELD ON OCTOBER 21, 1928, SHE was famous. Newsreels featuring her flight under the bridges would flash on movie screens around the world. Soon newspapers were filled with stories about the girl aviator.

She continued to soar, setting altitude, speed, and endurance records. In December 1928, Elinor challenged Viola Gentry and Evelyn "Bobbi" Trout to a duel—the longest flight wins. Elinor begged aircraft designer Giuseppe Bellanca to build a special plane with a 46-foot wingspan and 225-horsepower engine. No woman had ever flown a plane that powerful.

Circling Roosevelt Field in the Bellanca, Elinor read *Tom Sawyer*, ate sandwiches, and sang every song she could remember. Almost before she knew it, she'd flown twenty-six hours, twenty-three minutes, and sixteen seconds—over eighteen hours longer than Viola, and nine hours longer than Bobbi. Her record still stands today. Elinor and Bobbi became friends, and teamed up to become the first women to refuel a plane in flight. Fulfilling her dream to become a professional pilot, Elinor was named chief test pilot for the Bellanca Corporation. In 1930, at age nineteen, she was voted the best woman pilot in the United States by the nation's fliers, selected over Amelia Earhart as well as other women aviators like Louise Thaden, Phoebe Omlie, and Florence Lowe "Pancho" Barnes. Elinor wrote aviation columns in major magazines and hosted her own weekly radio program.

Elinor married, had four children, and took a break from the sky. She returned in 1956, piloting jets and flying paratrooper training missions with the Air Force Association. In 2000, at age eighty-nine, she became the oldest person to "fly" the NASA Space Shuttle Simulator. Young or old, Elinor has never forgotten the feeling of the wind in her face as she whipped through the clouds.

"Children must be allowed to dream and have a horizon to work toward," Elinor says. "For me there was only one path: I knew from age six that I wanted to fly. Flying was the very breath of life to me and I was successful because I loved it so much."

Soar, Elinor!

SOURCES

ELINOR AND HER SON, PATRICK SULLIVAN, brought her story to life by granting me hours of interviews and access to her vast collection of papers and photographs. I held her goggles to my face and wore her flight helmet. Swapping flying tips, pilot to pilot, with a flier as accomplished and venerable as Elinor was a dream come true.

But I also wanted to fly a plane like Elinor's, to experience the wind singing in the wires and the rumble of the engine, my hand on the stick and my feet on the rudder. Very few Waco 10s still exist, and most of the survivors are grounded as museum exhibits, never to fly again, but John Corradi and his antique Waco ZPF-7 still soar in Culpepper, Virginia. John, my ten-year-old son Will, and I flew loops and spins in John's graceful old bird. In the open cockpit I understood Elinor's consuming passion for the sky. Although John's plane is a bit younger than Elinor's Waco, it allowed me to experience firsthand how she stood in the cockpit to see over the engine cowling, and how she performed sideslips, then quickly turned her plane's nose forward to land.

Dr. John Kinney of the Aeronautics Division of the Smithsonian Institution's National Air and Space Museum advised me on technical matters, from control panel layout to the sound of a Farman pusher biplane's engine. The Air and Space Museum archives provided hundreds of newspaper clippings and magazine articles about Elinor Smith, as well as scrapbooks, correspondence, personal memorabilia, and files from the Department of Transportation concerning Elinor's quest for altitude and other records.

I read countless books and articles, including Elinor's own autobiography, to learn more about her and the other women in early aviation. These include:

Atkins, Jeannine. *Wings and Rockets: The Story of Women in Air and Space*. Illustrated by Dušan Petričeč. New York: Farrar, Straus and Giroux, 2003.

Boase, Wendy. *The Sky's the Limit: Women Pioneers in Aviation*. New York: Macmillan, 1979.

Moolman, Valerie. *Women Aloft*. Alexandria, Va.: Time-Life Books, 1981.

Smith, Elinor. *Aviatrix*. New York: Harcourt, 1981.

———. "This Business of Flying." *Liberty*, 9 August 1930, 30–40.

Smith, Helena Huntington. "New Woman." *The New Yorker*, 10 May 1930, 28–31.

Veca, Donna, Skip Mazzio, and Carol L. Osborne. *Just Plane Crazy: A Biography of Bobbi Trout*. Santa Clara, Calif.: Osborne, 1987.

The author gratefully acknowledges Toni Mullee, executive director of the International Women's
Air & Space Museum, for her expert reading of the manuscript.

Photograph of Elinor Smith and image of Elinor Smith's license from the National Aeronautic Association of U.S.A.
are reproduced with the kind permission of Elinor Smith. Photograph of plane flying under Manhattan Bridge © *New York
Daily News.* Photograph of Elinor Smith standing beside airplane © Underwood & Underwood / CORBIS.

Distributed in Canada by D&M Publishers, Inc.
Color separations by Chroma Graphics PTE Ltd.
Printed in May 2010 in China by Macmillan Production (Asia) Ltd., Kwun Tong, Kowloon, Hong Kong (supplier code 10)
Designed by Jaclyn Sinquett
First edition, 2010
10 9 8 7 6 5 4 3 2 1

www.fsgkidsbooks.com

Library of Congress Cataloging-in-Publication Data
Brown, Tami Lewis.
    Soar, Elinor! / Tami Lewis Brown ; pictures by François Roca.— 1st ed.
      p.   cm.
    Includes bibliographical references.
    ISBN: 978-0-374-37115-9
    1. Smith, Elinor—Juvenile literature.   2. Air pilots—United States—Biography—
Juvenile literature.   3. Women air pilots—United States—Biography—Juvenile literature.
I. Roca, François.   II. Title.

TL540.S64B76 2010
629.13092—dc22
[B]
                                                             2008030405